Wow! Look What Bugs Can Do!

KINGFISHER
LONDON & NEW YORK

Distributed in the U.S. and Canada by Macmillan,
175 Fifth Ave., New York, NY 10010
Library of Congress Cataloging-in-Publication data has been applied for.

Author: Camilla de la Bédoyère
Design and styling: Liz Adcock
Jacket design: Liz Adcock
Illustrations: Ste Johnson

ISBN 978-0-7534-7515-7 (hardback)
978-0-7534-7516--4 (paperback)

Kingfisher books are available for special promotions and premiums.
For details contact: Special Markets Department, Macmillan,
175 Fifth Ave., New York, NY 10010.

For more information, please visit
www.kingfisherbooks.com

Printed in China
1 3 5 7 9 8 6 4 2
1TR/0719/WKT/UG/140WFO

Wow!
Look What
Bugs
Can Do!

KINGFISHER
LONDON & NEW YORK

The bug club

Step into the exciting world of mini-beasts!
Don't be afraid!

Tsh-eeEEE-e-ou

We can be **noisy!**

Wow!

There are at least one million different types of insects in the world.

Male cicadas (say sic-KA-da) "sing" to tell female cicadas to come and visit them. They make their song by shaking a drumlike part of their body. They are so loud they can be heard 440 yards (400 meters) away.

We can be **strong!**

A mighty rhinoceros beetle can carry a load up to 850 times its own weight. That's like a human grownup carrying six full double-decker buses.

4

We can be COLORFUL!

The bright colors and eye spots on a peacock butterfly's wings scare birds away.

Eeeek!

Dinner time!

We can be fast!

Tiger beetles can run so fast they can't see where they're going! They can reach speeds of 6 miles per hour (9 kilometers per hour).

Blink and you'll miss me!

Wow!

All the ants in the world weigh more than all the humans. There can be 20 million ants in just one swarm.

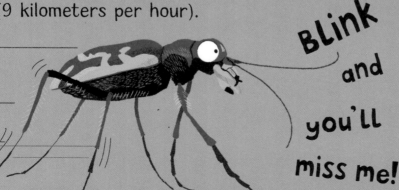

Onward!

A lot of legs!

Bugs slither, creep, crawl, scamper, swim, climb, crawl, or fly. Look how they move!

Insects have six legs and spiders have eight legs. Woodlice have 14 legs, but millipedes and centipedes have lots of legs!

I have no legs, but I have **one foot!**

Slugs and snails don't have any legs, but they slither along on a slimy body bit called a foot!

stop,

where are you going?

Caterpillars use their stubby little legs to creep along leaves . . . until danger strikes. Then they drop to the ground and roll away.

drop

Wow!
A grasshopper uses its powerful back legs to jump to almost 3 feet (1 meter) high!

and roll!

How does a desert spider avoid burning its feet on hot sand? It does cartwheels!

wheeeee!

Cartwheeling is a great way to escape hungry, stinging scorpions.

What's over here?

Wow!

Millipedes have a record-breaking number of legs—up to 750 of them!

Look at all my legs!

Best friends forever

The world needs bees! They are hard-working bugs that like to boogie!

Thousands of bees live together in a hive. It's packed with six-sided cells where the queen bee lays her eggs.

I'm the **queen bee!**

Yummy

Worker bees collect sweet nectar and pollen from flowers. They turn it into delicious honey!

Follow me!

A bee dances its own special boogie to show its hive-mates where to find the best flowers. It's called a waggle dance.

Clever death's-head hawk moths smell like bees. They can sneak into hives and steal honey!

You smell **good!**

If a hungry hornet invades the hive, the bees quickly gather around and shake their bodies so fast that the hive gets super-hot and the hornet flees.

Yikes, it's too hot for me!

Did you know?

When bees visit flowers, they pollinate them. That means the flowers can grow seeds, which will grow into new plants. Bees help plants grow, so we have fruit and other food to eat.

9

All change

A caterpillar doesn't stay a caterpillar for its whole life. It grows into a butterfly!

1 A caterpillar hatches from an egg and turns into an eating machine. A monarch caterpillar can eat 200 times its own weight in just 10 days!

1 Yum... yum... yum

2 Caterpillars spin a silk case around their body. It's called a pupa or chrysalis (say KRIS-a-liss).

4 I suck sweet nectar.

2 I'm ready for a nap now!

4 The pupa cracks open and a butterfly climbs out. Its wings are wet so it spreads them out to dry before it can fly.

3 Nearly ready!

3 Inside the pupa, the caterpillar's body turns into a souplike gloop. It then starts to grow into a new body, with wings, legs, and antennae.

The Queen Alexandra's birdwing butterfly is the largest butterfly in the world. Its wingspan can reach up to 10 inches (25 centimeters) across.

Look at my **HUGE** wings!

Mmm... I love poo!

Wow!
There are about 150,000 types of butterflies and moths.

A butterfly's tongue can be as long as its body. The tongue reaches into trumpet-shaped flowers to suck up the nectar.

Slurrrp!

Purple emperor butterflies don't feed on nectar—they prefer mud and poo!

11

Bugs everywhere

Bugs can live almost anywhere. They can live deep underground and have even been into space!

For 12 days, water bears zoomed through space in a rocket. They lived in extreme cold or heat, with no air, food, or water!

Hello from up here!

The Cooloola monster spends its whole life underground, so no one really knows anything about it!

I'm a mystery!

Barbecue time!

Saharan silver ants live in the Sahara Desert in Africa. They wait until other bugs fry in the burning sunshine, then gobble them up.

A family of fruit flies has its own home on the International Space Station! Scientists have sent bugs away from planet Earth to help the scientists learn how we could live in space.

Home, sweet home.

Wow!

Tapeworms live inside an animal's gut and feed on the poo there. They can lay 100,000 eggs a day. Gross!

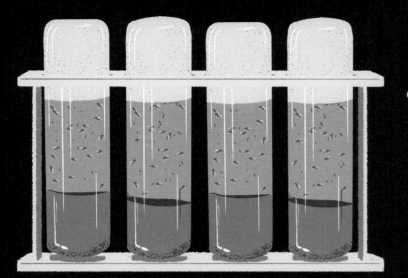

This Alaska beetle could live happily in a freezer! It lives near the icy North Pole and can survive in temperatures as low as −100 degrees Fahrenheit (−73 degrees Celsius.)

Move over!

Ladybugs huddle together in caves to survive a long, cold winter. A nest can have up to 40 million beetles snuggled up together.

Hide and seek

Some bugs have smart ways to stay off the menu.
Some are shy, but others love to be noticed.

This looks like a leaf, but look again . . .
it's a leaf insect. When an animal uses
color and pattern to hide from hungry
predators, it is camouflaged.

You can't see me!

Don't eat me, I taste bad!

Wow!

A leaf insect will also
sway left to right to
look like a leaf blowing
in the wind.

The spots on a ladybug
warn birds that it can make
a nasty-tasting juice ooze
out of its knees!

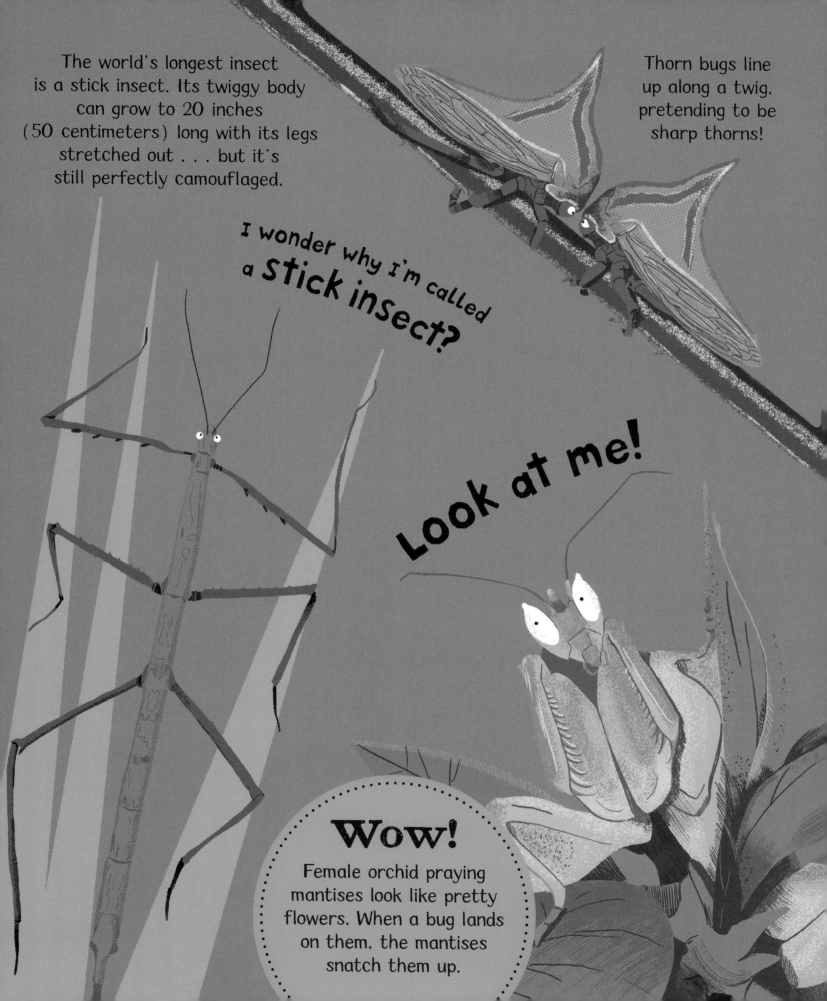

The world's longest insect is a stick insect. Its twiggy body can grow to 20 inches (50 centimeters) long with its legs stretched out . . . but it's still perfectly camouflaged.

Thorn bugs line up along a twig, pretending to be sharp thorns!

I wonder why I'm called a **stick insect?**

Look at me!

Wow!

Female orchid praying mantises look like pretty flowers. When a bug lands on them, the mantises snatch them up.

Super senses

Have a chat with a bug, it can hear you...
and also see you, smell you, and feel you!

Cicadas have ears on their stomach, crickets have ears on their legs, and spiders have thousands of little "ears" all over their body!

I'm a good listener.

Wow!

A spider doesn't have a nose or a tongue because it uses its eight hairy legs to taste and smell instead!

I spy, with my two enormous eyes...

Dragonflies have the best eyesight in the insect world. One eye is made up of 30,000 tiny eyes, called lenses, and each one sends a mini-picture to the bug's busy brain!

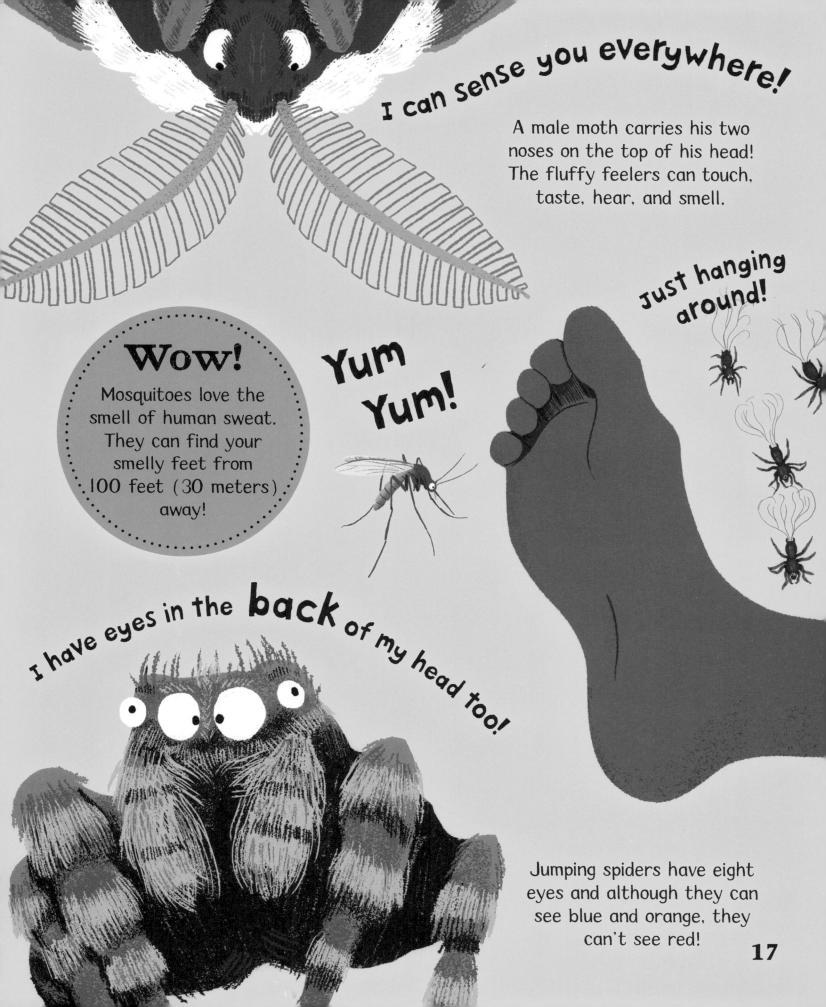

I can sense you everywhere!

A male moth carries his two noses on the top of his head! The fluffy feelers can touch, taste, hear, and smell.

Just hanging around!

Wow!

Mosquitoes love the smell of human sweat. They can find your smelly feet from 100 feet (30 meters) away!

Yum Yum!

I have eyes in the back of my head too!

Jumping spiders have eight eyes and although they can see blue and orange, they can't see red!

17

Scary spiders

Meet a ferocious family of fearless hunters! Are you scared?

Spiders have been around for at least 300 million years. They are hungry hunters with big jaws, a pair of mini-legs for touching and feeling, and eight walking legs.

We are definitely creepy...

...and crawly!

Did you know?

Spiders belong to the same family of bugs as scorpions, mites, and ticks—they are all called arachnids.

Wow!

The largest spiders are the size of a dinner plate, and are strong enough to catch and kill frogs and lizards.

These mini-monsters are mostly harmless to us, but they're deadly to other bugs. A spider uses long fangs to inject nasty venom into its victim, then vomits burning juices over it before sucking out the insides!

Spiders make silk. It's strong, stretchy, bendy, and sticky, so it is perfect for building webs.

we're super sporty!

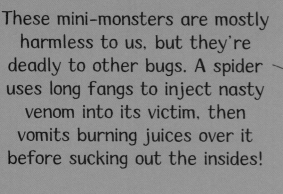

Baby spiders fly through the air on silk strands and can even use silk like a parachute to travel across land and sea!

My web is 6 feet (2 meters) wide and I can catch a bird!

What are you so happy about?

This spider is called a happy face spider. Can you guess why?

Colorful peacock spiders love to dance. They wiggle around to attract a mate.

Home sweet home

Small bugs have some big building skills!
They can create an impressive home.

Tiny termites use soil to build their homes. Termite mounds can be 33 feet (10 meters) tall, and are filled with tunnels and rooms—and thousands of termites!

Tap, tap!

These beetles make their home by eating it! Deathwatch beetles munch through wood to create tunnels and rooms. They tap the wood to let other beetles know where to find them.

It's a long way to the top!

Termites make great gardeners too. They grow their own food inside the mound.

Some spiders live in water. They build their underwater homes from silk and fill them with bubbles of air so they can breathe.

I'm a diving bell spider and I'm cozy and dry.

Wow!

Some bugs wear their home! A young caddisfly makes its home from sticks, stones, or leaves and glues it onto its body.

Peekaboo! Gotcha!

Eeeek!

Funnel web spiders dig tunnels and then cover them with a hidden trapdoor. They lurk inside and wait for other animals to pass by!

21

Brilliant beetles

Beetles are record-breaking bugs. There are over 300,000 known species!

The largest beetles can be bigger than a newborn puppy. The grub of an Actaeon beetle can weigh as much as two apples and you'd need both hands to hold it!

Time for a diet?

I can grow to **6 inches** (15 centimeters) long.

Watch out! A titan longhorn beetle can break a human finger with its giant jaws—but the biggest beetle jaws belong to the Grant's stag beetle. It could give your toes a nasty nip!

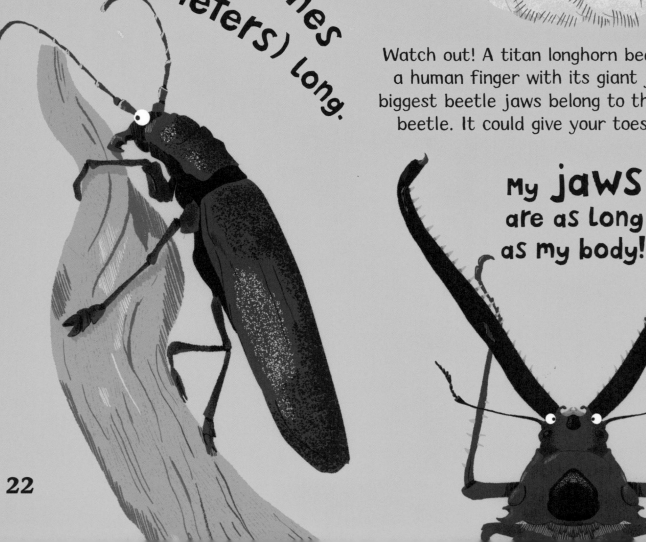

My **jaws** are as long as my body!

Some beetles are brilliant because they glow in the dark! They are called glow-worms or fireflies and they flash lights in the night to find each other!

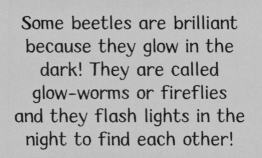

I have a flashlight for a bottom!

I'm SO shiny!

Jewel beetles are shiny and colorful. They are so beautiful that people used to turn them into jewelry.

Ready, steady ...

Wow!

A bloody-nosed beetle spits out a big blob of its own foul-tasting blood when there's a scary predator nearby.

23

Super survivors

Bugs have some amazing ways of staying alive—and some wicked weapons.

...BANG!

When a bombardier beetle is under attack, it turns into the world's most explosive insect. It fires a puff of burning gas and liquid out of its behind!

A praying mantis sits very still until it sees its prey. It then speedily grabs its victim in its mighty, crushing claws. It can launch an attack in less than 0.01 seconds!

snip, snap, crunch!

Wow!

Cockroaches are super survivors. If one loses its head, it can still live for months even though it can't eat or see!

Scorpions curl their long tail over their head to sting a victim. Deathstalker scorpions have enough venom to kill a human!

LOOK out!

I'm a f-ant-astic mini-monster!

Ants can bite, sting, or spray burning acid. A bullet ant attack is said to be one of the most painful stings in the world.

Stinky!

Stink bugs are a juicy treat for birds, but they make a foul stench when they spy a feathered fiend!

Splish! Splash!

Water bugs

Not all bugs live on land. Look below the water to spy some swimming bugs.

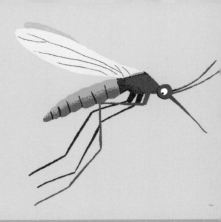

Giant diving beetles are big enough to eat small fish, and when they are scared by big ones, they produce a foul liquid.

Adult mosquitoes lay their eggs in water. When they hatch, little larvae emerge and hang from the surface of the water.

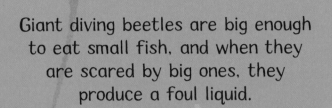
Look out fish! We are diving down!

Wow!

Some bugs can breathe underwater, but others swim to the surface to grab a bubble of air. They carry the air on their hairy belly or under their wings.

Can you do the backstroke like a water boatman? This insect swims upside down and uses its hairy legs like long oars to paddle around.

Just keep swimming...

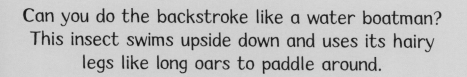

Wow!

A dragonfly nymph lives in the water for around four years. It then grows wings, turns into an adult dragonfly, and flies away.

Hurry up, wings! I want to fly!

I'm a soup-er slurper!

The giant water bug is a powerful predator. It can grow as big as your hand and it stabs fish with a daggerlike mouthpart. Its poisonous spit dissolves its victim's flesh, so it can suck it up like fish soup!

What a pest!

Lots of bugs are good news for us and the environment. But some are troublemakers . . .

There can be 80 million locusts in one swarm. Together, they can gobble up 423 million pounds (192 million kilograms) of plants in just one day.

I've got **79,999,999** friends!

Wow!

A bark beetle is the size of a grain of rice, but billions of them live in trees and they can kill whole forests.

Awesome ants march in huge gangs—20 million driver ants can trek right through farms and villages, eating crops. Luckily, they also eat other pests such as cockroaches.

Keep up! We're on the move.

28

Ouch!

Most spiders have a bite that is harmless to humans, but some have deadly venom. Bites from black widow spiders, Australian funnel web spiders, and brown recluse spiders can kill.

Mmmm! Humans. My favorite!

Blood-sucking mosquitoes are the mostly deadly bugs in the world because some of them spread a horrible illness called malaria (say mal-AIR-ee-a) when they bite their victims.

Left, right, Left, right.

Kissing bugs like to bite people around the mouth. They can carry a disease that makes humans ill.

Give me a Kiss!

That's so gross!

Feeling hungry? Bugs can have some really icky ways of feeding.

A burying beetle buries a mouse and covers it with stinky goo to stop it from rotting. The female beetle lays its eggs by the mouse so the maggots have fresh food to feast on when they hatch.

Anyone seen a dead mouse lying about?

Shall we dance?

No thanks!

Tick tick

A tiny tick is a mini-monster. It bites into flesh and sucks up the blood. As it feeds, a tick squirts its spit into a wound, and that spreads diseases.

Some female bugs make a meal of their mate! Praying mantis moms often bite off their mate's head!

Dust mites live in beds where they feed on dead skin. Each person sheds enough dead skin in a day to feed a million dust mites, and up to 3 million dust mites live in a bed!

Night, night!

Bedtime

Bedbugs live in mattresses and come out at night to bite the humans sleeping there. They feed on human blood. Thankfully, most beds don't have bedbugs in them!

I love bugs!

I'm saving you for Later.

Help, I'm stuck!

Some frogs have a smart way of catching a bug lunch. They cover their skin with sticky goo. Biting ants quickly discover their jaws get stuck to the goo, but can't escape. The frog sheds its skin and eats it, along with the juicy ants!

31

Bugs in danger

We need bugs—the planet depends on them!

Without ants, there'd be no anteaters...

Bugs are food for many animals and they help plants grow. Without them, people and animals would starve.

Please help us.

There are many threats to our precious bugs. Chemicals that kill bad bugs kill the good ones too. Many wild places where bugs live are being destroyed or damaged.

The Ceylon rose butterfly is in danger of extinction because its forest home is being cut down.

Don't squish bugs!

Ladybug spiders are very rare and may die out forever. Their grassland home has been destroyed to build houses and farms.

Did you know?

Did you know how important bugs are? Spiders eat flies that spread diseases, worms keep the soil healthy, and bugs that eat poo, dead animals, and plants are nature's recyclers!